Elephants

Elephants

Part one

Elephants in the Animal World

This portrait of a large male African elephant exudes power coupled with a look of wisdom passed down from time immemorial.

African elephant, master of the bush

The African elephant is the largest land mammal on the planet. Its strength, power and incomparable physique make it a unique animal. This giant, with its sometimes touchy nature, reigns over the savannah with no enemies in the animal world.

Groups of elephants walking peacefully and unafraid amidst other animals in the African savannah.

The African elephant, like its Asian cousin, is a representative of the order Proboscidea, animals with trunks. These two animals are the last survivors in this group. The African elephant, larger and stronger than its Asian relative, is the world's largest living land mammal. Its dimensions speak for themselves: adult males are between 2 and 3 metres tall at the shoulder, with an average length of 7 metres from the tip of the tail to the end of the trunk. Large males weigh

The savannah or bush elephant is the largest of the two African elephants.

Apart from its imposing bulk and ivory tusks, the trunk is undoubtedly the elephant's most original feature. It can be used to pump up water for drinking.

The elephant's trunk, which can be used as a dexterous and powerful 'hand', is equipped with tens of thousands of muscles. It is useful for both drinking and eating.

The second subspecies of African elephant lives in the forest.

up to 7 tonnes; while females are smaller they still make imposing mates.

The trunk, an all-purpose organ

Besides their large ears and highly developed ivory tusks, African elephants have a completely unique organ in the form of their trunk, which ends in two mobile and very agile 'fingers'. This sensitive, powerful appendage enables the elephant to pull up a tree or pluck a piece of fruit. It uses its

The curve of the tusks varies from one elephant to another. They are covered by a layer of enamel which protects the ivory when the tusks clash in greeting.

▼ The elephant has very unusual dentition. It does not use all its molars for chewing. Those that are put to work wear down and eventually fall out and are then replaced by other teeth. Their lozenge-shaped imprint – loxodonta in Latin – gives the African species its scientific name, Loxodonta africana. The tusks, the upper incisors, grow throughout the elephant's life and are used for digging in the earth, breaking branches or stripping bark off trees, and when necessary for confronting enemies.

trunk to trumpet, drink, caress, greet its fellow-elephants and sniff the air to determine the weather – in short, to live its life as an elephant.

Some old elephants sport superb inward-curving tusks.

Large ears of various shapes

A head lit up by two small bright eyes, the yellow-brown or reddish iris of which is constantly moving, is framed by two huge ears. The wide ears, often bearing the marks of many scars, are an identity card unique to each individual. They are very mobile and serve as fans in the heat of the African bush. The elephant opens them out completely before making an intimidating charge. Finally these outsize appendages can detect very low frequency sounds, enabling elephants to communicate amongst themselves at distances of up to 5 kilometres.

From the virgin forest to the African bush

In former times the primary virgin forest was probably the African elephant's main natural environment. While there are still a few elephants living in the equatorial jungle today, most of the herds are to be found in the savannah. The forest elephant, which is becoming extinct, is slightly slimmer than its grassland counterpart. Its ears are smaller, enabling it to slip through the depths of the jungle without catching them too much. The ivory of its tusks is tougher so that it can strip the bark off large hardwood trees. In the savannah the bush elephant's tusks enable it simply to dig the ground in search of water. The bush elephant is a good walker and travels much farther than the forest elephant, which does not have such long distances to cover in search of food.

Elephants never pass up an opportunity for a nice mudbath.

A glutton with an insatiable appetite

Elephants are big eaters, an adult taking in between 150 and 380 kilograms of food daily depending on the season. They eat mainly grass, leaves, small branches, tree bark, roots and fruit. Furthermore they are not averse to swallowing earth which is rich in mineral salts. They round off their meals in this way, avoiding any dietary deficiencies. With a diet such as this, eating occupies about 20 hours out of the elephant's day. To hydrate their huge bodies

Elephants go to extremes to look after their skin, bathing with water, mud or dust; they initiate their young into these cosmetic practices at a very early age.

Though the elephant's skin is rough and thick (pachyderm comes from a Greek word meaning 'thick-skinned') it is very sensitive. An elephant taking a bath is always a spectacular sight in the life of the savannah. Mudbaths in particular are essential for their hygiene. The mud cools, maintains and softens their skin – elephants have no sweat glands or sebaceous glands to do this naturally. As it dries, the mud forms a solid shell which destroys any parasites on the skin.

under the relentless African sun they also need to drink nearly 100 litres of water daily. Therefore looking for a water hole is vitally important and can drive herds of bush elephants to travel several hundred kilometres. If necessary they are capable of going without a drink for several days, provided their food is still rich in moisture.

Three guests sharing the same table round off their meal with some earth.

Matriarchal herds

Elephants lead very structured social lives. The females and their

No plant escapes the elephant's appetite; it will even swallow acacia thorns.

Water is essential to elephants, both for drinking and for bathing.

The search for food keeps elephants busy all day.

offspring live in herds, while the adult males live alone or in very small groups Thus the largest elephants herds are always controlled by an old female. The senior female takes on the role of mentor, managing the entire life of the clan. As the guardian of her herd she defends the other elephants with great courage in the face of danger. As First Lady of the herd, the matriarch is entitled to the respect of the other females, who prove their devotion by following her blindly in all things.

When danger is imminent the females of the herd surround the elephant calves and wait for a signal from their senior – she decides whether to flee or to face the enemy.

In the fine season elephants wander across the grasslands of the savannah.

The size of the clans and their travels

In former times large African troops consisted of several thousand elephants. Nowadays the largest herds can be counted in tens. In areas where food is abundant (forest areas or the savannah in the rainy season) the herds of elephants do not move far. Temporary groupings bring together small families that are geographically close. In the driest zones (the Sahel or the savannah in the dry season) and when pasture is scarce, the

On their migrations elephants follow traditional routes. That is how the memory of each herd is expressed.

The African elephant with its outsize dimensions has found a tree worthy of it: the baobab which provides a far from negligible food supplement in the dry season.

groups break up into small units consisting of only one or two females and their young. The small, mainly family groups are then forced to wander as nomads over long distances, following paths that remain identical from one year to the next. When living conditions in the wild once more improve, bigger communities re-form, and the animals rejoin their large original group. With their legendary memories, elephants always remain loyal to their initial ties.

This apocalyptic scene indicates that a herd of elephants has passed through.

The elephant's anger can be terrible. A large angry male charges, his ears unfurled, to intimidate or perhaps even crush his enemy.

The forest elephant treats every part of the tree as food.

Solitary males

Driven out of the clan at puberty to prevent them from mating with cow elephants from their own herd, 11- or 12-year-old males in turn group together to form small bands of bachelors. These never go above about ten individuals. The still adolescent male elephants lack experience and stay close to the herd of females that raised them, but now unceremoniously rejects them. Once they are fully adult (more

Elephants often meet up at the edge of the river.They like to cool down there and if the need arises they can be quite good swimmers.

Large males also suffer during the dry season and are forced to travel huge distances to assuage their thirst.

Once aged over 30, males have no option but to lead a solitary life, returning to the females only when in rut. This large male walks alone with a confident step.

than 25 years old), males lead an increasingly solitary existence on the periphery of the herds. In their prime there are never more than two or three males wandering about together. They tend to be rather temperamental animals, and range over the huge spaces of Africa passing through the territories of several clans. The oldest males live an extremely solitary existence; abandoned and alone in the world, they die far away from their families.

In old age these giants turn their backs on life and die alone.

In the dry season food becomes scarce for elephants. When there is a shortage of grass, they compensate by eating more wood.

Finding a partner

When the urgent desire for love makes itself felt (each bull elephant has a rutting season individual to him), males actively seek the compliance of females who are on heat. Cow elephants are receptive throughout the year, with a menstrual cycle of about two months, and have no preferred season for giving birth. Thus by going from one group to another, males looking for a mate will always eventually

In arid zones elephants dig deep down until they reach water.

The carefree calf elephants, serenely protected from danger by the females of the herd, roll on the ground and enjoy the pleasure of being caressed by their mothers.

These two bachelor males are travelling together.

strike lucky. But this search does have the effect of making them somewhat aggressive, and all animals on the savannah, human beings included, treat these giants with caution when they are looking for a partner. Furthermore, the abundance of food which influences the cow elephant's fertility is a factor in regulating the birth rate. In normal conditions a female elephant gives birth every four to five years.

Male elephants sometimes live like hermits, meeting their fellow-elephants only by chance, when their paths cross.

Cow elephants have to suckle their young for two years.

The infancy of calf elephants

The elephant's calves are born in a fairly rough and ready way, falling on to the ground as they emerge from the womb – cow elephants give birth standing up. The newborn calf immediately attracts the attention of members of the herd who greet its arrival by sniffing it with their trunks. Calf elephants are precocious, being able to walk just after being born and learning to

Once he has found the ideal partner, after fondling her at length, the rutting male mates with the female. He covers her for barely 30 seconds.

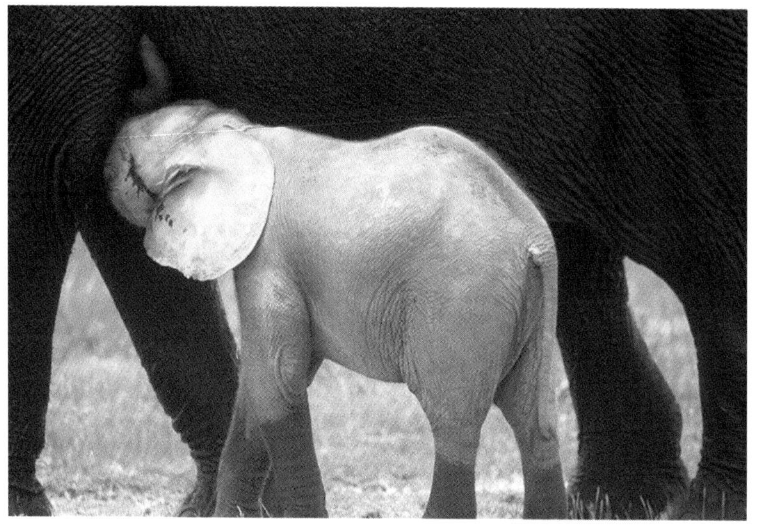

Calf elephants spend their childhood at their mothers' side, playing happily and learning.

suckle from their mothers just as quickly. Weighing over 100 kilograms at birth, small elephants grow steadily until the age of four, putting on 10 to 20 kilograms each month. They grow up surrounded by their elders who teach them the rules of the group's nomadic life.

Cow elephants show great affection towards one another.

With a few rare exceptions, Asian elephants have tusks that are relatively or completely undeveloped. In all cases tusks are found only on males of the species.

Asian elephant, a giant in the forest

The largest animal on the continent of Asia is the Asian elephant. Like its big cousin in Africa, this pachyderm is a colossus. It lives only in the forest, rarely has tusks and in spite of its vast size is decidedly less irascible by nature.

Asian elephants live in forests. Less tolerant of heat than their African cousins, they appreciate the shade afforded by the branches of the trees.

The Asian elephant differs from its African cousin in its more rounded outlines. It is also smaller and lighter: 3 metres tall at the shoulder for an adult male which can weigh up to 5 tonnes. Female Asian elephants are no taller than 2.5 metres and weigh barely 3 tonnes. There are other fundamental differences between the African and the Asian elephant: the latter has a forehead with two bumps and a thin scattering of hairs, framed by small ears.

In spite of its small eyes, this Asian colossus is very sharp-sighted.

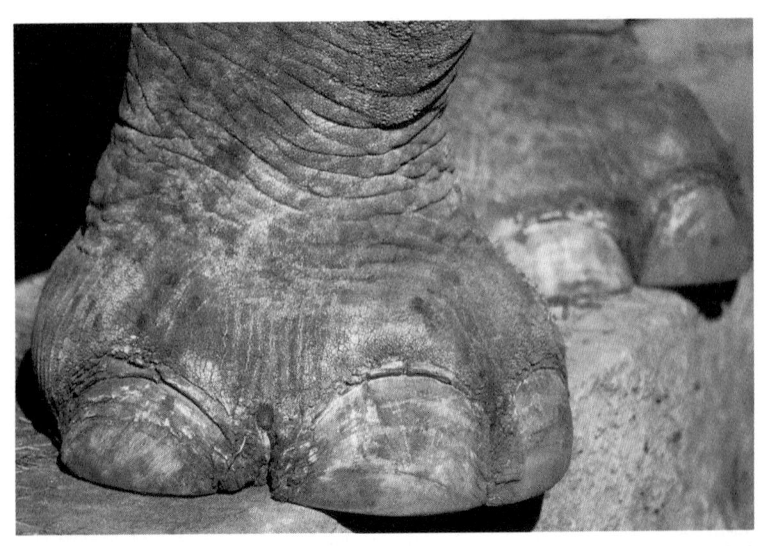

The front legs of Asian elephants have five nails while the hind legs have three or four. A pad of tissue inside the foot acts as a shock absorber.

The Asian elephant's long, heavy trunk can become a powerful weapon when it comes down on an enemy's head. The animal also raises it to greet a fellow elephant.

Young Asian elephants are often very hairy. The hairs are brown or black.

A well formed head

In the case of the Sumatran elephant, one of the four subspecies of the Asian elephant, these small ears are almost square, and it is quite hard for the ears to regulate the temperature of a large body that is none too keen on the intense heat and burning rays of the sun. The eyes of all Asian elephants – small, with a brown-red iris, and constantly moving – are protected by large eyelids. The Asian elephant is also decidedly

Asian elephants sometimes use their tusks as a 'trunk-rest'.

hairier than the African one, the Malaysian elephant being particularly hairy: its Latin name is *Elephas maximus hirsutus*.

A universal appliance

The trunk of the Asian elephant ends in a single 'finger' whereas the African elephant's has two. This all-purpose appendage – it is used for pumping up water, spraying it over themselves, browsing from a distance, lifting tree

Asian elephants loves swimming. Neither running water nor sea inlets can stop them. They then use their trunks like a tuba for breathing.

When their trunks are not rolled up, Asian elephants use them to probe, sniff and explore every square inch of unknown territory before stepping on to it with their feet.

trunks, giving caresses – is sometimes so long that the animal rolls it up so as not to get its feet tangled up walking on its nose. The Asian elephant's fragile skin, grey-brown in colour, some-times has light patches on some parts of the body as a result of loss of pigmentation. This tends to become more marked with age, showing up mainly on the head, trunk and ears. That is enough to explain public belief in Asia in the myth of white elephants: if not pink ones!

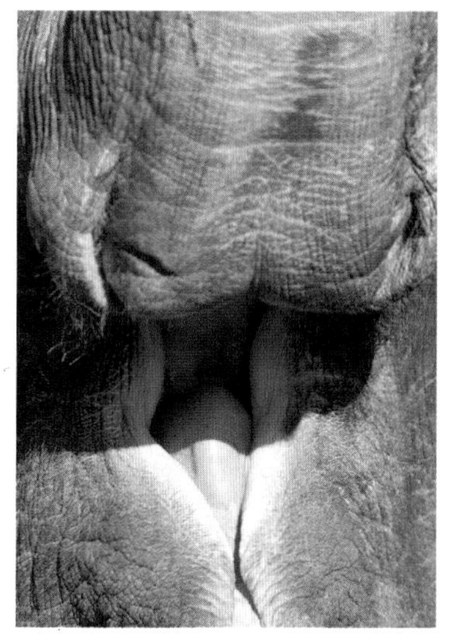

The female of the Asian elephant very rarely has tusks.

No tusks or virtually none

Asian cow elephants do not have tusks, or only exceptionally. In the extremely rare cases when they do, their tusks are tiny compared with those proudly sported by large African females. Asian males also have smaller tusks than African ones. In the case the special subspecies that lives in Sri Lanka (Elephas maximus maximus), only one in every ten bull elephants has tusks.

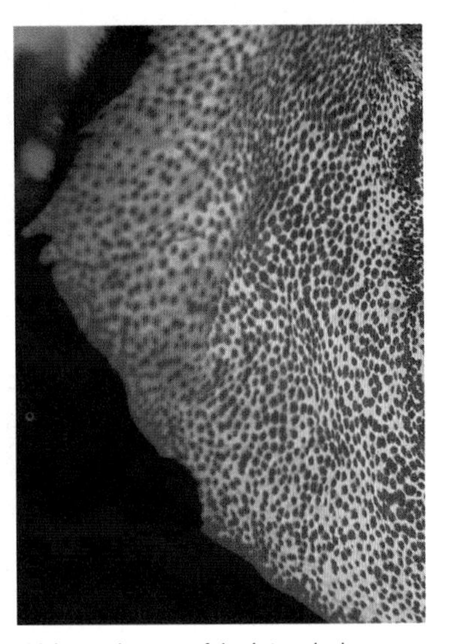

With age, the ears of the Asian elephant lose their pigmentation.

A loyal forest dweller

The Asian elephant, a natural forest dweller, lives in all forested areas on that continent, from the humid tropical forest to the grassy jungle by way of drier forest. It has thus become acclimatized to very different places. For example, in the Himalayan chain some elephants nip about at the snow line, the limit of the everlasting snow. Still demonstrating their climbing skills, but under more clement skies, they can be found in the heart of the mossy jungle in Java or Sumatra islands, ascending the impenetrable slopes of volcanoes up to 3000 metres high. These gentle giants, ambling along,

In the jungle the Asian elephant is light-footed and can move without making any noise. It is possible for a big male weighing nearly 5 tonnes to leave no tracks on the ground!

The elephant's digestion takes place in the intestine, not in the stomach. The micro-organisms in the intestine enable it to transform the cellulose of the plant matter into molecules that can be assimilated. The passage of food through the intestine being faster than in ruminants, the elephant can ingest large quantities more rapidly. The elephant calf which is born without these essential micro-organisms acquires them through absorbing grass soiled with dung or by directly swallowing its mother's dung.

demonstrate an incredible sense of balance however steep and uneven the ground, and are equally at home travelling in the mountains or crossing plains interspersed with trees.

Great connoisseurs of the plants of the forest

The diet of Asian elephants is similar to that of their large African cousins, involving very large meals consisting of grasses, roots, bark, wood, fruits and earth!

Crossing a river affords the ideal opportunity to take a shower.

Waterholes are an important element in the life of the Asian elephant. Not only for drinking and washing, but also for meeting up with other members of the herd.

In the jungle, bull elephants cover more ground daily (up to 30 kilometres) than herds of cow elephants accompanied by their young.

A hungry bull elephant can swallow more than 300 kilograms of plant material in 18 hours. The fermentation of the fruit ingested can make the animal drunk.

In the forest, elephants belonging to one herd always use the same paths to the various water points.

Marshes form a habitat much enjoyed by elephants.

On average adults consume a minimum of 150 kilograms of fresh plant material daily and drink 100 litres of water to keep in good shape.

An ecologically minded destroyer

Asian elephants are discerning gourmets, particularly enjoying delicate bamboo shoots for their tenderness and the leaves of wild fig-trees. But to vary their everyday diet they can sometimes also eat sugar cane

Elephants sleep very little, and are on their feet from dawn, taking their family breakfast in the jungle mists.

Calf elephants can digest only the most tender branches.

and rice – they will emerge from the forest to visit human plantations, causing terrible havoc as they pass through. However, in spite of this dark picture, these apparently destructive giants play an active role in preserving their own environment. As they do not digest all they take in, they evacuate half of what they have swallowed intact. Thus the large quantities of dung left along their tracks are rich in an incredible variety of seeds. By spreading all these seeds in manure that promotes their germination and at a distance from where they were swallowed, elephants make a big contribution to the natural renewal of the plants in their environment.

The elephant's trumpeting is a prelude to flight or attack.

Their memory of secret trails

In southern Asia elephants faithfully follow the paths taken by their ancestors and which they have followed for several generations. Depending on the variable terrain,

Elephants' proverbial memories enable them to remember the paths they have followed, the places where they have grazed and those where they have been in danger.

The elephant's skin has a great many tiny creases which make ideal nests for parasites. A dust bath is one of the measures it uses to rid itself of them.

The newborn elephant is about a metre tall and weighs about 100 kilograms. Up until the age of six months, and sometimes even three years, the Asian calf elephant sucks its mother's teats with its mouth, raising its trunk. Elephants' milk has a higher fat content than cows' milk, and is runnier. Young elephants can also take solid food, but are as yet unable to 'prepare' it. It is the adults who bundle up the grass, or crush tough branches to make the nurseling's job easier.

Calf elephants are very curious and playful.

they are also capable of following the crests of mountains and the relief of the land without ever having to come down. They then enjoy a panoramic view of the jungle which helps them find their bearings. In the heart of the impenetrable virgin forest, they thus mark out virtual corridors – runs – which are then also used by other wild animals such as tigers or buffalo. Sometimes this network of natural tracks even enabled humans to build roads, as happened in the Assam region of India.

Close families under the trees

In the depths of the Asian forests the cow elephants and their young form very united communities. When food is plentiful these wild herds tend to become sedentary. If for any reason members of the group separate for some time, their reunions are joyful, noisy and very emotional. The bull elephants are rather apart, approaching this female environment only when they are in rut, which often happens at the height of the rainy season.

The principle of mutual help within a group of elephants enables them to overcome many obstacles.

When they are in rut adult males are aggressive and always ready for a fight.

The love life of elephants

During the mating season adult males will travel through the forest in every direction, rending the air with their raised trunks and criss-crossing through the trees. They are desperately in search of receptive females. Once contact has been established, long preparations get under way during which the cow elephant guides her partner. The male mounts his mate for

Cow elephants remain within the same family unit, their own herd, throughout their lives. They play a part in protecting and educating the boisterous young.

just 30 seconds, and 22 months later a baby elephant weighing about 100 kilograms is born. Within a few hours the calf elephant is on its feet. Two days later it can walk and follow its mother, holding on to her tail to avoid getting lost. Until it reaches a fair size a calf that loses its way in the forest is in fact in great danger – the danger of meeting a tiger, it's only mortal enemy which does not fear the elephant until it is adult.

The survival of the calf elephant depends on its mother and the rest of the herd.

During the glacial stages of the Great Ice Age the cold was not the mammoths' only enemy. These gigantic animals covered with thick fur were to disappear some time later.

Ancestors, and unexpected cousins

The African and the Asian elephant are the last survivors of a distinguished line, the order Proboscidea. From mastodons to mammoths, all these giant animals with trunks have disappeared from earth, but they still have some unusual relatives, such as manatees and dugongs.

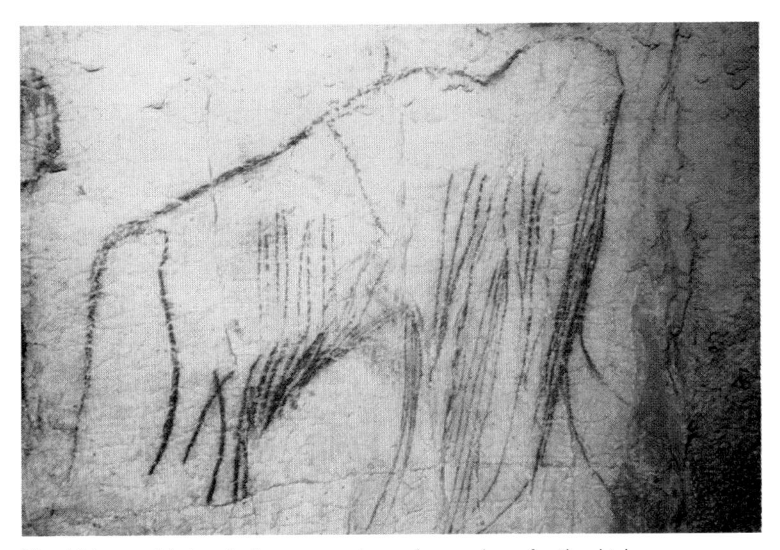

The African and Asian elephant are orphans of a once large family which was widespread on every continent. They now bear witness to a very early past.

Once upon a time there were proboscideans, which can be roughly translated as 'animals with a trunk'. The story of the planet's last giants started nearly 50 million years ago when Moeritherium saw the light of day.

The shadow of the elephant's vanished ancestors still hangs over mankind.

A very small ancestor

Moeritherium, which must have been similar to a tapir with hippopotamus's feet, lived in the north and west of Africa. Its fossil remains were discovered in the early 20th century on the

While proboscideans can manifest very different physical characteristics, they do have one shared feature – the trunk.

The term 'mammoth' was coined at the end of the 17th century by Dutch explorer Witsen. Of Siberian origin, the exact etymology of the word remains unknown.

The elephant's first known ancestor no doubt looked like a tapir.

shores of Lake Moeris (Egypt), hence its name. With its relatively undeveloped or even non-existent tusks, it would today cut a small and ridiculous figure alongside its last descendants. It is the oldest known ancestor of the elephants.

The birth of a trunk, the death of some species

Before disappearing completely, however, Moeritherium had time to engender several families which grew larger, then were

Like life, nature can be surprising. The strongest animals are not necessarily the ones that are best adapted to surviving in hostile environments.

The elephant's powerful trunk is also its 'Achilles' heel'.

scattered in the course of time. Their representatives gradually put on weight while an exceptional organ started to develop, and become immoderately long: the trunk, proboscis in Latin, which was to become the predominant attribute permanently distinguishing their faces. It is an atavistic characteristic and became their distinctive mark. Most species descended from Moeritherium are now extinct, leaving posterity with the names of distinguished lines such as the mastodons, stegodons and Elephantidae: the most outstanding members of the latter family are mammoths and present-day elephants.

The most famous relation: the mammoth

Of all prehistoric animals, it is mammoths that fire our imagination most. The first mammoths in fact made their appearance three million years ago. In Europe they lived in the bush and in forests, in the steppes and the tundra, while other different species were evolving in North America.

Elephant ivory is the same as fossil mammoth ivory.

Prehistoric pachyderms had the same good-natured look as their cousins the elephants. The latter have survived, and still display the same good humour.

The best-known member of the mammoth family is the woolly mammoth (Mammonteus primigenius) which lived on the continents of Europe, Asia and America. We are familiar with its appearance thanks to the many frozen carcasses found in Siberia and Alaska and drawings made by human beings in the Stone (Paleolithic) Age.

Mammoth fossils have made it possible to write the history of elephants.

An animal clad in a fur coat

Comparable in size to the present-day African elephant, the strange woolly mammoth was perfectly adapted to the extreme cold then prevalent in these areas. It was in fact covered with a thick, brown-black, woolly fleece which enabled it to endure, in at least relative comfort, the climatic rigours of the glacial stages of the Great Ice Age. The enormous head, crowned with an attractive, very thick tuft of hair like a Russian fur hat, supported a pair of incredibly well developed, upward-curving tusks that could be up to 5 metres long. A fatty hump on the nape of the neck served as a food store during hard winters.

Animals descended from Moeritherium have changed a lot.Three members of this large family are Palaeomastodon, Mastodon and the mammoth.

Hunting mastodons was a far from restful business. To exploit the huge quantity of meat men first had to conquer their own fear.

In Siberia there are real mammoth cemeteries. Important remains, either frozen, or preserved to a greater or lesser extent by the frost, have in fact been found there. A great many tusks have been picked up among the bones. Moreover the longest tusk ever found belonged to a woolly mammoth and is held in a museum at Brno in the Czech Republic. It measures 5.02 metres round the outside curve. Another tusk belonging to an imperial mammoth was unearthed in Texas in the USA. It is over 4.9 metres long.

The disappearance of the mammoths

A dead mammoth could make a whole village happy.

Although adult mammoths were huge awe-inspiring animals with no enemy other than humans, their young were at the mercy of the large predators of the period. Among these, the sabre-toothed tiger was a fearsome enemy that was very widely distributed over the planet. It was found both in Europe and Asia as well as in Africa and America. The tiger's exceptionally well developed upper

Once killed huge elephants more than satisfy human needs. All parts of the animal can be used by human beings.

Our fascination with mammoths has withstood the test of time. Thanks to the magic of cinema these huge proboscideans come back to life before our enraptured eyes.

In the bush the African elephant, the largest living land mammal, walks in its ancestors' footsteps. It is the keeper of the Proboscidea memory.

The Asian elephant is a cousin of the African elephant. But in the fight against their own extinction the two large animals stand as brothers, and touch trunks.

canine teeth were exceedingly effective, but their voracious appetite alone does not explain the disappearance of the mammoths, which occurred about 10,000 years ago. Scientists have reached agreement on two points – firstly, the intensive hunting practised by prehistoric humans would have led to the slaughter of many of these long-haired animals; secondly, mammoths which were adapted to the cold would have suffered dreadfully from the warming of the climate. Heavy snowfalls and thaws

The mammoth was a favorite prey of sabre-toothed tigers.

The story of evolution is often full of weird and wonderful surprises, revealing the fascinating differences between species.

flooded pasture land, creating hardship for the herds. The weakest died first, while the strongest, which were also the heaviest, risked sinking to their death with every step they took. To add to this tragedy, the reproductive cycle of the female mammoth was particularly slow and a species that could not make up its losses was destined to disappear, particularly as the dangers of mating on the unstable ground – skidding, and even greater risks of sinking – were also against them.

It is hard to imagine that the tree hyrax is distantly related to the elephant.

Hyraxes are only found in African.

Very strange distant relatives

If the elephant diaspora ultimately established elephants in Asia and Africa, the last giants with trunks still have a few terrestrial cousins such as the daman, or aquatic ones such as the manatee or the dugong.

Little terrestrial brothers

The daman (or hyrax), a direct descendant of Moeritherium, is a small furry herbivore belonging to the order Hyracoidea. Nowadays they

Rock hyraxes, or damans, live in south-east Africa, Sinai and the southern Arabian peninsula. They are exclusively saxatile, leaving their hiding places to find food.

Damans, related to proboscideans and sirenians, are similar to marmots. The daman's name comes from the Hebrew word 'Saphan' meaning 'one who hides'.

The legend of the sirens is often associated with manatees, but it would seem that Homer was referring to dugongs. The dugong, like the manatee, is a marine mammal belonging to the order Sirenia, and it too is related to the elephant. The dugong is usually smaller and lighter than the manatee; it has softer skin and a pair of little tusks which begin to emerge after puberty. Their limbs are better adapted to marine life than those of the manatee, and they are found along the coasts of the Red Sea or the China Sea.

Tree hyraxes, or damans, are excellent climbers; they live in the African forests.

are found only on the African continent and in the Middle East. In spite of this reduced geographical territory there are three distinct types, tree hyraxes, bush hyraxes and rock hyraxes. They rank as featherweights, ranging between 1 and 6 kilograms, and not exceeding 60 centimetres in height. All these animals share the following features in common with their big brothers the elephants: they have flat nails and forward-pointing upper incisors that continually grow, forming tiny tusks which they uncover when threatened. Rock hyraxes and bush hyraxes live in small communities made up of a few adult females, one adult male and young of both sexes. As with elephants, young males are driven out of the family clan at puberty.

The manatee: a generously proportioned siren

The other unexpected relation of the elephant is the manatee, an aquatic mammal belonging to the order Sirenia, also known as the 'sea cow'. It in no way resembles our image of a siren. In fact, its fat, massive,

The manatee, a streamlined aquatic mammal, has no external ears or hind limbs. Its forelimbs enable it to move along the water bed.

fusiform body, smooth skin, hairless except for several bristles on its snout, rounded head with no external ear, forelimbs transformed into flippers and wide tail acting as a rudder do not conjure up the superb, legendary anatomy of the sirens who seduced Ulysses' sailors in days of old.

The manatee relies on its flat rounded tail for swimming.

A fragile life that is under threat

Manatees are adapted to an aquatic life spent in fresh or

Slowly and peacefully, the manatee drags its huge bulk through the water.

brackish water, and still live in the large rivers in Africa and America and their estuaries, in shallow lagoons and in swamps where fresh water and sea water mix. They are exclusively herbivorous, browsing on floating or underwater plants throughout the day, consuming on average about 30 kilograms of plant material daily. The manatee is a protected species, but human beings with their motorboats are still its main enemy, other than crocodiles and sharks which savour its tender flesh.

The manatee feeds on mangrove leaves, water hyacinth and other invasive plants. Its intestines are as large as those of its relative, the elephant.

Part two

Elephants in Our World

Through the ups and downs of history the African elephant has carried the weight of the past on its back, bearing witness to human behaviour towards it.

A symbol and a game animal

In Africa the elephant was hunted for food long before people became interested in it for its ivory. Its exceptional size meant that it occupied an important place in the various different African civilizations. The elephant is a living symbol.

The flesh of elephants was used for a noble cause: human survival. But the ivory from their tusks is endangering them now because of human greed.

Elephants are overshadowed by the threat of the extinction of the species.

On the continent of Africa, elephants and human beings have long been at odds. That is why, despite its powerful symbolism, the indomitable African elephant has always been preferred dead rather than alive.

A food source

Throughout Africa this formidable animal was once killed for its meat. A single slaughtered beast could provide a generous food supply for a whole village for

The traditional way of hunting elephants is with bows and arrows.The trap is often to immobilise the elephant in a ditch so that it can be more easily hit.

Cutting up an elephant lying on the ground is like a woodcutter's work because the skin is so thick and tough.

several days, and apparently its delicate meat has a similar flavour and consistency to beef. So as well as providing protein for peoples who often suffered famine, elephant meat made a contribution to the flavours of traditional cooking.

Even nowadays some African villagers still eat elephant meat.

A high-risk hunting technique

Elephants were usually hunted with lances, arrows serving only as a back-up. This method of hunting is fairly risky, requiring a

Among some peoples in Gabon the killing of the elephant is preceded by magic ceremonies orchestrated by the nganga djoko (master of the elephant rite).

Romain Gary's novel The Roots of Heaven provides an illustration of the relationship between the elephant and human beings: 'When Africans have full stomachs they may start to take an interest in the aesthetic aspect of the elephant and take time to meditate pleasurably on the beauties of nature in general. Meantime nature advised them to slit the elephant's stomach and sink their teeth into its flesh, eating and eating until they could eat no more, because they did not know where their next meal would come from.'

The elephant's strength is not always sufficient defence against hunters.

large number of hunters to attack the elephant together. Thus the Hottentots, a nomadic people inhabiting the west of South Africa and Namibia, start by cutting one animal off from the group. They then harass it, using dozens of their poisoned arrows to wound it. Once it has been weakened it still has to be finished off using a lance.

The art of camouflage

The Pygmies, very good hunters who inhabit the equatorial forest, use a similar technique, but one where camouflage plays a major part. They smear themselves with elephant dung to mask their own scent, so duping their future victim. In the heart of the forest the cautious animal is then at the mercy of the hunters who can now approach really close to it with their iron-tipped spears. They then slip underneath the animal and slit its stomach. Among the Pygmies this ambitious slaughter, where the important thing is to avoid being crushed, is something of an initiatory test in which young hunters can fully demonstrate their virility and courage. In other forest-dwelling tribes, elephant hunters are strictly forbidden from indulging in sex

The wardens and vets in African National Parks are often helpless in trying to deal with poaching by all those who kill elephants for their tusks.

Ivory tusks are trophies that are proudly displayed by hunters.

before setting off on a hunting expedition. The elephants would take flight immediately they detected female scent. For all these peoples it is not only the meat of the elephant that is of interest: its hide, hair and above all its tusks are used to make breastplates, jewellery and musical instruments.

The elephant cemetery

The fascination ivory holds for human beings has played a large part in giving

According to many legends and stories passed down by the elders to their descendants elephants hide themselves away to die, as if through a sense of discretion.

rise to the fabulous myth of the elephant cemetery. According to this there was a secret, inaccessible place where old elephants in their death throes went to die, leaving eternity to care for their tusks. The discovery of strange places where large deposits of bones were found fed the legend. But let there be no mistake about it, these huge sites were the result of the period when colonial settlers used their guns to carry out mass slaughters of elephants. From the late 19th century to the

Drastic measures are required to protect African elephants.

In certain African countries there are sometimes too many adult bull elephants in the National Parks. Generally the governments decide to cull them.

Watch out for wild animals in South African parks.

end of the 1970s elephants were the victims of virtual 'genocide', solely to obtain the ivory from their tusks and provide fleeting glory for the greedy hunters.

Murderous fires

Another theory regarding the existence of elephant cemeteries was based on the idea that whole herds had been trapped by bush fires during periods of drought. Encircled by flames, the large animals supposedly perished in the fire, whereas ivory hardly burns.

Elephants are a threat to crops, provoking the farmers' anger. Sometimes they are prone to getting stuck in muddy marshland.

The former kingdom of Bénin used to trade ivory with the Europeans, especially the Portuguese, depicted on this salt cellar.

Myths, stories and magic

As well as being seen as high-value game – the ivory market was very lucrative – the elephant's image in traditional African society was often that of a heavy, gullible and sometimes clumsy creature. However, the creature has great symbolic importance throughout the continent. According to Baule belief, in the Ivory Coast, the elephant represents longevity, prosperity and wisdom, even if other ethnic groups see it as

Ivory is a precious material to use to make this handle for a fly-whisk

For the Bamileke in Cameroun, tusks are a symbol of wealth.

In Cameroun, beautiful elephant masks are worn for festivals.

In the town of Mombassa in Kenya there are monumental arches shaped like elephants' tusks. Perhaps they bring luck to the cars passing underneath them.

representing only violence and ugliness. In Benin the teeth and bones of elephants are believed to have magic powers and are used as powerful talismans by the marabouts. In addition to these magic powers extraordinary curative virtues are attributed to the elephant's blood and skin. Thus they are reported to have been used successfully in medicines for the treatment of leprosy, the plague or scurvy. Elsewhere there is no better relief for migraine than a fine elephant's trunk on one's head.

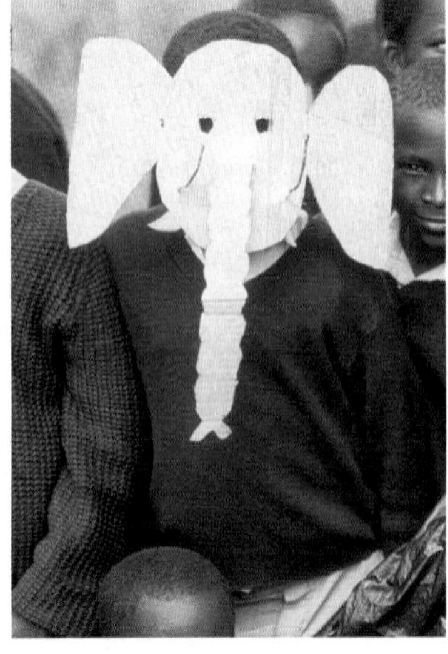

African children become aware of the elephant's importance at a very early age.

In spite of a ban on the export of untreated ivory in most African countries, carved souvenirs can still be found in tourist gift shops.

Bracelets made of hair from the elephant's tail are lucky amulets.

In other villages, for example in western Africa, the elephant is regarded as the most perfect creature ever to exist. Finally, there were sacred areas throughout the continent of Africa where elephant hunting was strictly forbidden.

A giant scared by a mouse

These ancient beliefs and taboos are dying out, but bush stories are still told to children. Thus the elephant has inspired many African fables, including a tale from Gabon entitled 'Father elephant recounting how the elephant that was frightened of nothing and nobody ended up being terrified by a little mouse'. The animal had laid waste to the manioc and millet fields belonging to the village, and to get rid of the elephant the villagers tried to oppose it with animals likely to scare it off: a leopard, a crocodile, and a snake, three champions that the bellicose elephant had easily seen off by crushing them. Fortunately the village mouse, the last resort to counter the destructive giant, approached the elephant while it was asleep and gnawed the skin on its feet. When it woke up, the disabled elephant refused to believe that such a small animal could have caused it such pain and viewed the mouse as a powerful demon possessed of tremendous magic powers.

In 1992 the Rio summit reaffirmed the protection of threatened species.

The giant tricked by the hare

Another well-known myth that is widely told in the bush features the elephant and the hare. One day Hare gets married. But he is too lazy to clear the sorghum field that the new couple will need to live on. He decides to employ cunning and thinks up a

Working with ivory requires great precision and a lot of patience.The talent of some African ivory workers has raised simple craftsmanship to the status of true art.

Ivory has always fascinated human beings. Having been used in early times to make tools, in the course of the centuries this 'white gold' became a noble material usedby artists. And the fine tusks of the African elephant became a sought-after prize. The slaughter of elephants has been reduced only very recently, with the signature of an agreement between more than a hundred countries in 1989 banning all trade in ivory. Although the African giants have been saved for the moment, there is still a great deal of poaching.

Rock carvings of elephants can be found in the wadis of the Sahara.

trick which involves using the strength of the two largest animals in the bush to do the work in his place. Hare claims to be stronger than Elephant, and challenges him to a tug of war. He makes the same proposal to Hippopotamus, ties the two mastodons together and leaves the two heavyweights to pull, each thinking that Hare is at the other end. Thus Hare's trick snares Elephant and Hippopotamus, in other words, the ultimate symbols of strength.

In the savannah the hare always achieves its objectives by means of cunning. In African stories the elephant is as often as not the victim of the long-eared, fast-running hare.

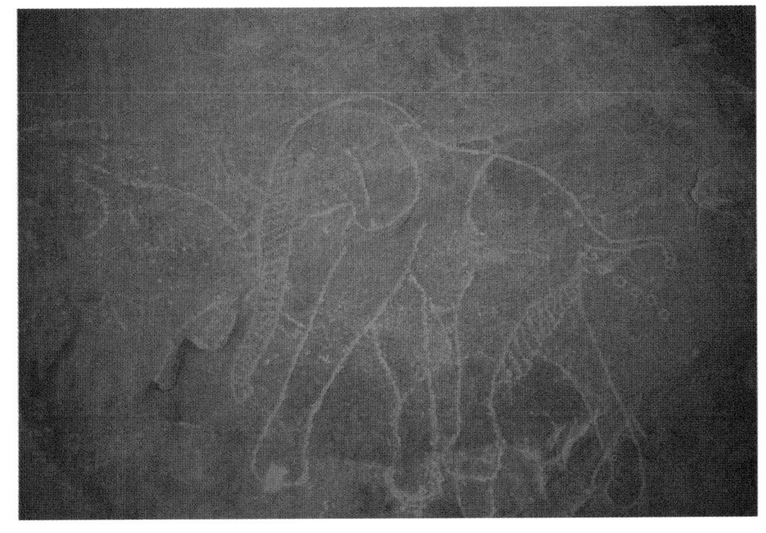

The rock carvings depicting the elephant in the Algerian Sahara, at Tassili for example, are nearly 5000 years old. Some details are quite realistic.

Elephants carved in ebony are popular souvenirs with tourists.

In the beginning was rock painting

In Africa, people also used the elephant as an aesthetic image, demonstrating their artistic abilities. Prehistoric 'artists' drew the elephant. Rock paintings of elephants found in the heart of the Tassili National Park on the rocks of the Sahara bear witness to earlier times when the desert was savannah strewn with trees. Human beings and beasts then lived together.

The image of the largest land animal is used in the decoration of the Sun City hotel complex in South Africa.The elephant's presence can be seen throughout the site.

The rising popularity of World Music since the start of the 1980s has enabled African musical groups to be heard on the largest international stages. The Zénith concert hall in Paris, for example, has hosted the Touré Kounda. Originally this group was formed from the members of one family which took the figure of the elephant as its emblem. In Africa it is fairly common for an animal to be associated with a family name because of its qualities: strength and wisdom in the case of the elephant.

The Elephants, a Côte d'Ivoire football team, have very colourful supporters.

An ever-present image

Elephants inspired those first African artists, and their image still has an exotic or naive appeal today. Thus carvings of elephants in ebony and a range of craft items are produced for tourists in Africa. As a symbol of strength and longevity the elephant also appears on many African banknotes, as if it could impart some stability to national currencies.

The elephant in all its states

African musical expression has also appropriated the image of elephants, in particular in the form of the Senegalese group Touré Kounda, whose name translates as 'elephant family'. Where sport is concerned, the elephant's awe-inspiring appearance and invincible nature have been taken up by the national teams of the Ivory Coast, their football team in particular. Thus each year when the African Cup is held, the Ivory Coast Elephants prepare to charge the Mali Eagles or the Cameroon Lions, even if the rules of the sport are not necessarily the same as those of the bush or the jungle.

In Asia the deified elephant sometimes takes on a very far-fetched appearance, and the ways it is depicted always include some poetic licence.

A god in Asia

In Asia humans and elephants have long coexisted peacefully. Considered the equal of the gods, the elephant is viewed as sacred and worshipped. Domesticated 5000 years ago, the docile Asian elephant was the mount of princes – in hunting and wars – and is a powerful draught animal.

In a world where human beings and elephants enjoy a fairly good understanding, it is not uncommon to observe scenes where they keep one other company and merge.

Asia established a special relationship with its elephants at a very early stage. They were considered sacred and deified, occupying a prime position in both the Buddhist religion and the Hindu pantheon. In civilian life they lent human beings their strength for their major projects.

In India there are many temples dedicated to Ganesa.

When the Asian elephant is tamed, it is so close to man that it can be regarded as an attentive friend, a loyal and powerful helper.

The elephant is the ideal motif to represent the pillars and foundations supporting temples, or simply to decorate some parts of a building.

In the beginning was the elephant

At the birth of the world, Brahma, the god who created the universe in the Hindu religion, also created Airavata, the ancestor of the elephants and the first being to emerge from the god's originating shell. Its powerful legs would be the four pillars that supported the weight of the universe. At a later stage the mount of Indra, the Hindu deity who presides over thunderbolts and war, would also be an elephant.

Ganesa is a god who is given star status during huge popular festivals.

In Jaipur in India elephants' owners organize beauty contests. The huge animals covered with brightly coloured floral motifs parade all through the town.

Every year the anniversary of Ganesa's birth gives rise to a huge festival celebrated by Hindus throughout the world. In Bombay effigies of the elephant-headed divinity invade the town and are worshipped for three days in the houses and streets. Offerings of food are made to them as Ganesa is a very greedy god. These piles of foodstuffs are then taken to the shores of the Indian Ocean and cast on the waves where they sink along with Ganesa.

The birth of a Hindu star: Ganesa

In Hindu mythology the elephant head of the god Ganesa is the result of a dreadful tragedy. A very long time ago the goddess Parvati, the wife of Shiva, gave birth to her first child, Skanda. She experienced such joy that sacred milk spurted forth from her breasts. Mixing this divine nectar with the sandalwood ointment she spread over her body, the goddess fashioned her second child Ganesa, and entrusted him with guarding her palace. In his zeal Ganesa prevented even the god Shiva from entering the dwelling of his own wife. Shiva was overwhelmed by a terrible rage and immediately beheaded the stubborn youngster. Cast into despair by this barbarous act Parvati then threatened to destroy the entire universe. To assuage his wife's anger Shiva promised her he would borrow the head of the first creature that passed near the palace and put it on the body of the god child. An elephant was walking nearby and ever since Ganesa has had his definitive form, the head of an elephant and a child body.

Ganesa is a popular god who plays a very important role in everyday life.

Sitting in his niche, the god Ganesa displays his rounded stomach.

Ganesa, a likeable and popular god

With his rounded stomach and kindly air Ganesa is an appealing figure. Protecting the home and bringing good luck to businesses, he can often be seen in shops and above the doors of houses. Ganesa is also the god of study and writers; he is the symbol of knowledge and Indian students call on him to pass their exams. Finally Ganesa expresses the

The god Krishna kills an elephant in a fearful rage. This god is a warrior prince as well as an ardent lover who enjoys round dances.

idea that human beings and the universe exist in perfect symbiosis. This smiling god is always accompanied by his favourite mount, a mouse. The strength of the elephant is thus associated with the dexterity of the tiny rodent, a unique union calculated to overcome all the obstacles of life.

In Hindu mythology the first elephant was the guardian of the universe.

How beautiful Maya gave birth to the Buddha

The elephant also plays a fundamental role in Indian

The palace of Jag Mandir belonging to the famous Emperor Shah Jahan is one of the treasures of Udaipur, the City of Dawn, a town in Rajasthan in northern India.

The sacred white elephants of King Bhumibol of Thailand are looked after with special care. Most Thai people believe they bring peace and prosperity.

Buddhism which is the basis of all other forms of Buddhism. Thus one fine summer's night Queen Maya, a very beautiful virgin, was visited by a white elephant. The animal entered the royal bedroom delicately bearing a lotus flower in its trunk. Nine months after this experience the virgin queen gave birth to the Buddha in the tranquil gardens of her palace. From that time on, the white elephant has been worshipped in South-East Asia.

The sacred elephant is carrying a venerated relic: the Buddha's tooth.

Once a year the Perahera takes place at Kandy or Colombo in Sri Lanka. It is a night-time religious procession when the Buddha's sacred tooth is displayed to the people at large.

In Bombay in India the festival of Ganesa gives rise to a huge, colourful celebration during which there is constant popular excitement for three days.

The strange appearance of the white elephant, has always been believed by those living in South-east Asia, to have magic powers.

The anniversary of the birth of Ganesa is celebrated every year in September.

His majesty the white elephant

The white elephant, which is actually light grey, is the object of a cult in Laos, which used to be called the 'kingdom of a million elephants', Myanmar (formerly Burma) and Thailand. For all the Buddhists of these countries albino elephants (extremely rare specimens affected by a generalized loss of pigmentation) are regarded as reincarnations of Buddha.

The Perahera procession requires long, detailed preparations.

They are accorded every honour and the utmost attention is lavished on them. In Myanmar the white elephant is fed with the finest food served on gold and silver dishes. Some women even have the immense honour of suckling a white elephant calf. Furthermore, according to Myanmar legend, awhite elephant carrying a relic of Buddha (a tooth) chose the site for the large pagoda of Shwedagon in the capital,

At Trichur in the state of Kerala in southern India elephants caparisoned with gold bring reconciliation on the occasion of the Pooram, the only Hindu festival uniting all castes.

For a long time Asian peoples used to tame elephants to use them in war. If they were well trained these giants could carry several soldiers on their backs.

In Thailand there are reconstructions of battles between the Thai and Burmese.

Rangoon. In Thailand the white elephant has long been used as a symbol, appearing on the former national flag, and even today many Thai people liken the map of their country to the elephant's head. As the supreme sacred animal, a white elephant here belongs to the king and represents the country's well-being and prosperity. So one of the greatest honours in Thailand is the 'Order of the White Elephant'.

A formation made up of a few dozen war elephants could make a charge and break through the enemy's first fortified lines, so defeating him.

Whether intended for war or for hunting an elephant always needs long training and requires costly care. The daily upkeep of a princely mount gives it all its prestige and value. The elephant decked in gold and silver is a superb ceremonial animal. Nowadays the main religious feast of Sri Lanka, the Esala Perahera, is held annually at Kandy. A procession of about a hundred elephants through the town is led by an old male carrying a sacred relic on his back: Buddha's tooth.

The flamboyantly decked elephant bears the sacred tooth of the Buddha.

A war machine and fighting beast

In India the Hindus' sacred Vedic texts also conjure up the elephant as an animal of war. The traditional army of India consisted of the cavalry, the infantry and elephants, used in attack to break up the enemy's front line and create havoc in their ranks. In the 16th century the great Mughal emperor Akbar owned about 6000 fighting elephants. He used this fearsome army to cross the Ganges and invade and subdue the region of Bengal. Moreover, at that period conflicts between rajahs and princes were common. Differences were then settled by elephant intermediaries: the confrontation between two champion fighting el-ephants wearing body armour decided the victor. In times of peace everyone in this society enjoyed going to arenas where elephants had to fight tigers, a very colourful spectacle which delighted young and old alike. People also went tiger-hunting on elephant-back.

A beast of burden and a logger

As mounts, elephants carried out many other services. During World War II the Japanese used them in Burma to carry or pull artillery equipment. In places where motor-driven transports grind to a halt, elephants can get through without difficulty. In the forests of Thailand or Myanmar these great animals work as loggers, providing valuable assistance in bringing out teak. They fell the trees by butting them

Elephants are docile, and carry out the heavy labour in the forests of Asia.

In Sri Lanka conflicts between the Tamils (Hindus) and the Singhalese (Buddhists) have not spared the elephants. Wounded or orphaned elephants are cared for here.

At Surin in Thailand a gathering of elephants takes place every year. The large crowds that come to see them can admire the acrobatic feats they perform.

The felling and transport of wood is hard work and a proper job for elephants.There i a forestry training school at Lampang in Thailand.

Pacifist monks sometimes travel on elephant-back.

with their heads. Once the trunks have been cut into logs the elephants carry them with their trunks. However, in spite of all their qualities elephants have to be used sparingly, as they do not have great stamina.

Small by nature

An adult elephant can drag two tonnes of wood, but its carrying capacity is relatively low considering its own weight: just 500 to 600 kilograms, which is scarcely more than three

An outing on elephant-back makes it possible to admire the landscape.

times the load carried by a dromedary or a camel. The elephant is constantly required to lower itself and stand up again during its work in the forest, and as a result it tires rapidly. So these four-legged workers enjoy privileges not accorded to human beings: a five-hour working day, a siesta and a bath in the afternoon, and a drink whenever they want it.

An attraction for tourists

When not working, Asian elephants are used to carry

Cow elephants perform various tasks in forestry work, but it is the bull elephants which have tusks that carry the logs.

tourists inside reserves and parks. They are naturally easygoing, with an ambling gait and an innate sense of balance that seldom fails. However, they offer their passengers only relative comfort, and you have to be willing to accept a bumpy ride if you travel on an elephant's back. This job is less tiring than logging and animals assigned to it can work for six to seven hours a day.

Men may be fanatical about football, but elephants play too.

Elephants of leisure

In Nepal elephants also play a role in human leisure, serving as mounts for a 'heavyweight' version of polo. This use respects the tradition of the elephant as a noble mount. The players, tied to the animal's back and seated behind the mahout who is responsible for directing the beast, try to push a wooden ball into the opposing team's side using a long-handled mallet. Every year the impressive championship organized by the World Elephant Polo Association in Nepal brings together elephants and sportsmen from about ten nations for games on a phenomenal scale.

While polo is usually played on horseback, it can also be played on elephant-back. The players and animals act as one. In spite of their weight elephants can be agile.

▼ Despite the important role elephants play in Asian countries, the species is under threat. At the start of the 20th century their numbers there were estimated at over 100,000 animals. Today the population in the wild is no more than 40,000 to 50,000 individuals, nearly half of them in India, mainly in the north-eastern regions. The sharp rise in the human population of India has led to an increasing number of conflicts between human beings and wild elephants, driven out by deforestation and agriculture.

Dumbo, the famous elephant with the flapping ears, learns to fly. The West and the cinema were probably inspired by a Hindu legend relating to flying elephants.

A star in the West

In Europe and America the elephant first amazed people, then delighted them, and finally enjoyed a stunning success, culminating in its huge popularity today. From ancient times to the present day its history has combined exoticism with a certain romanticism.

The wars between Carthage and Rome in the third century BC were distinguished by the extraordinary epic of Hannibal and his elephants, crossing the Pyrenees.

Charlemagne's nephew Roland had an oliphant, an ivory horn used in war.

In bestiaries dating from Antiquity the depiction of the elephant very soon became a constant feature, even if it was sometimes fairly weird or something of an approximation. Later on it sunk into oblivion before gradually regaining its popularity over the centuries. Since then, what with royal menageries, colonial adventures, the great hunts in tropical countries, zoos, circuses, books and the cinema, the elephant has never left the limelight.

The Malatestas, a family of Italian condottieri who reigned over the town of Rimini from the 13th to the 15th century, built a temple there decorated with elephants.

On the forecourt in front of the Musée d'Orsay in Paris there is a sculpture by Emmanuel Frémiet (1824–1910) representing a young elephant.

A short history of the elephant

It seems that the Greek historian Herodotus in the fifth century BC was the first to give the pachyderm the name *Elephas*, meaning 'ivory'. Later on the Roman writer Pliny the Elder (first century AD) mentioned elephants in his turn in his *Historia Naturalis*. He asserted that the African elephant, being 'smaller' than the Indian one, could not bear to be seen by it,

Herodotus is often regarded as the 'father of history'.

and he reckoned that these strange animals could live to be 200 to 300 years old. Scientific knowledge of the elephant may have been at a rudimentary stage, but a few details are provided that parallel our knowledge of the elephant today. Thus Pliny notes that elephants live in groups, led by the eldest animal. Furthermore, this very early zoologist also refers to war elephants.

The Greek philosopher Aristotle saw the elephant as a symbol of fidelity.

The battle between Alexander the Great and King Poros in 326 BC subsequently contributed towards turning elephants into terrifying and powerful weapons of war.

Animals are central to the Fables of La Fontaine (1621–1695). In the fable 'The rat and the elephant' the large animal is mocked by the little one because it is slow.

In France the harbour town of Dieppe was a real centre of ivory from the 16th to the 20th century. This Venus was carved by Belleteste in the 18th century.

Alexander, the Macedonian conqueror, subdued the largest towns in Asia Minor, then after founding Alexandria in Egypt he reached the gates of Babylon.

Alexander (356–323 BC), a brilliant pupil of Aristotle, was destined for greatness.

Alexander the Great and war elephants

In 331 BC Alexander the Great was victorious against the king of Persia. As part of his loot he brought back ten or more Asian elephants. A few years later Alexander, eager for further conquests, fought the Indian king, Poros, on the banks of the Indus where Poros had assembled nearly 200 elephants. The battle ended with success for Alexander's armies.

Thanks to Alexander the Great's victories over the Persian leader Darius, then the Indian king Poros, war elephants gradually became familiar to artists of the period.

Hannibal (247–183 BC) gave elephants an important strategic role.

According to legend, both King Poros's elephant which defended its master valiantly and Alexander's famous horse Bucephalus died in the course of the desperate struggle.

Hannibal's elephants

Elephants also played an important role in the conflict between the Carthaginians and the Romans in the third century BC. They took part in the second of the three so-called Punic Wars, started

Charlemagne (742–814) was given a surprising present: an elephant.

by the Carthaginian general Hannibal in 218 BC. He had decided to disrupt the power of Rome by carrying the fight to Italy. Setting off from Spain with 36 elephants, Hannibal had to overcome a first difficulty: the Pyrenees. Several further obstacles, the river Rhône then the Alps, were crossed by the intrepid general and his elephants. Hannibal's campaign in Italy was a success, and the elephants helped to shatter the enemy lines.

In the Second Punic War Hannibal lost the Battle of Zama in 202 BC to the Romans commanded by Scipio Africanus. The elephants were handed over to the victor.

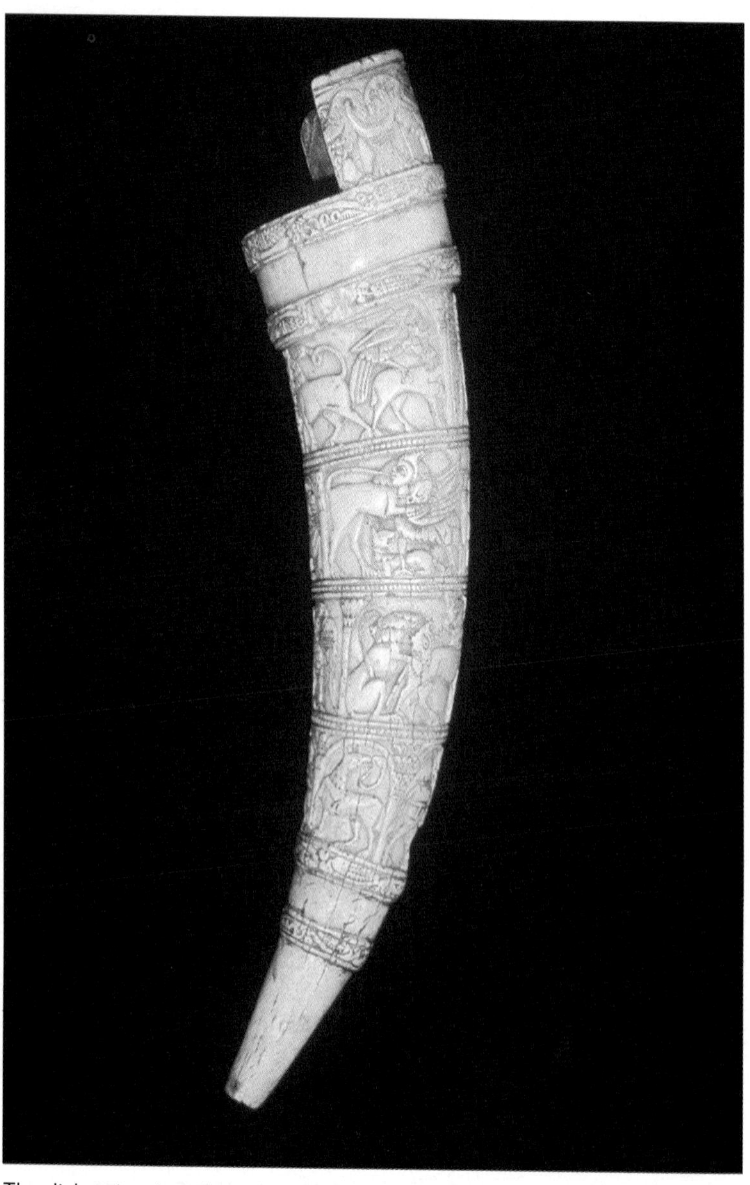

The oliphant is an ivory horn carved from an elephant's tusk. In a battle against the Saracens Roland refused to sound the oliphant to alert Charlemagne.

The elephant, an exotic gift

The 'gigantic' aspect of elephants has long captured the imagination of Old Europe. Because of their exoticism they have appealed to kings and those with enquiring minds throughout the ages. Thus Charlemagne received the gift of an elephant from the caliph Harun al-Raschid, a famous ruler of Baghdad who wanted to be on good terms with the Emperor in the West. In the 13th century the French king Louis IX gave

Pierre Graillon (1807–1872) made skilled ivory carvings like this one.

The war elephants captured by the Romans after their victories were taken back to Rome where they were often exhibited in the arena, like lions or bears.

In the West zoos, menageries and circuses developed during the 19th century, with elephants quickly taking pride of place.

The elephant is a figure that has inspired monuments. In Paris town planning gave rise to huge, far-fetched projects: an elephant fountain with rooms in its innards in the middle of what is now the Place de l'Étoile, or the Bastille elephant, the 'strange monument' inhabited by the urchin Gavroche, a famous character in Victor Hugo's Les Misérables. On the Piazza della Minerva in Rome stands the elephant created by the sculptor Bernini (1598-1680). This little monument is nicknamed 'the Minerva chicken'.

Henry III of England an elephant brought back from the Crusades. Four centuries later Louis XIV, the Sun King, was given an elephant at his palace of Versailles, a gift commensurate with his image of grandeur.

The elephant with an obelisk on top of it in Rome is by Bernini.

Myths and talismans

Besides its image as an exotic animal, the elephant in Europe has also been the object of various beliefs and superstitions. The people of Antiquity attributed virtues such as piety to the elephant, saying that it expressed all the respect due to the stars. Thus in the morning it hailed the sun with its trunk, while in the evening it paid homage to the moon, waving branches gathered in the forest towards it. According to Aristotle, who credited it with chastity and fidelity, the elephant had even taken vengeance on adulterers! Other beliefs are still current today. The elephant in the form of a piece of jewellery is supposed to promote wise decision-making provided the trunk is pointing upwards, while if it turns down, the item of jewellery will bring its owner

Sometimes elephants in zoos and circuses become dangerous, then their keepers have to kill them. This is what happened to Fritz, an elephant in Barnum's Circus.

misfortune. Receiving the gift of a ring or bracelet made using the hair from an elephant's tail mounted on a gold band is indicative of future prosperity. Finally a chance meeting with an elephant on emerging from a wedding service is supposed to be a very good omen.

Ivory and magic potions

As for ivory, its whiteness is a symbol of purity and its hardness a sign of power. Writers as early as Pliny the

The Éléphant brand of tea in France conjures up remote, exotic places.

Elder commented on the curative properties of ivory, protecting the body from certain illnesses. It was also a long-held belief that a mixture of powdered ivory and goat's blood would provide relief for pain of any sort and that ivory shavings mixed with honey would make freckles disappear.

The elephant, a circus star

It was in the largest big tops of the American circus that the elephant embarked on its career as an international

In the United States the elephant is a symbol of the Republican Party.

The ivory carver sitting at his bench uses many tools, generally made by himself. In his workshop the ivory carver Souillard is working on a statuette with an engraving tool.

artist. Already regarded as major attractions in Europe in the menageries and zoos of the 18th and 19th centuries, elephants would receive the ultimate accolade from the public in the United States with Barnum's Circus and Jumbo, a star among stars.

Colonel Hathi is the venerable elephant in the film, *The Jungle Book*.

The elephant in films and advertising

In 1941, drawn by Ben Sharpsteen and produced by Walt Disney, the elephant made its cartoon debut in *Dumbo*. In Europe the adventures of Babar, King of the Elephants, had started still earlier – the character was created by Jean de Brunhoff in 1931. Since then Babar has successfully transferred to the small screen where he delights young television viewers. In 1932 elephants also won the heart of Hollywood in the film *Tarzan the Ape Man*. They cropped up again in 1953 in *The Greatest Show on Earth*, a spectacular in the great tradition of the American cinema. Since then, elephants have broken into the world of advertising and fashion, an unparalleled achievement for an animal with such a girth!

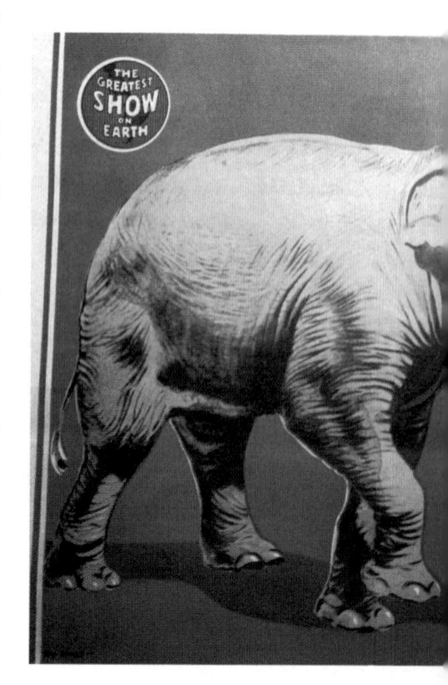

Babar has adorned the pages of strip cartoons, burst out of television screens and he could be found in wooden toys so he could carry on delighting children.

The most famous elephant in Barnum's Circus was Jumbo, a giant African elephant. As a distinctive feature of London Zoo, Jumbo was the pride and joy of England when Phineas Taylor Barnum disembarked there in 1882. A showman with a gift for recognizing a potential attraction, Barnum offered the sum of $10,000 to buy the elephant. In spite of the disapproval of the English public, Barnum took Jumbo back to the United States where the animal and its owner received a triumphant welcome.

ELEPHANTS

in Africa and Asia

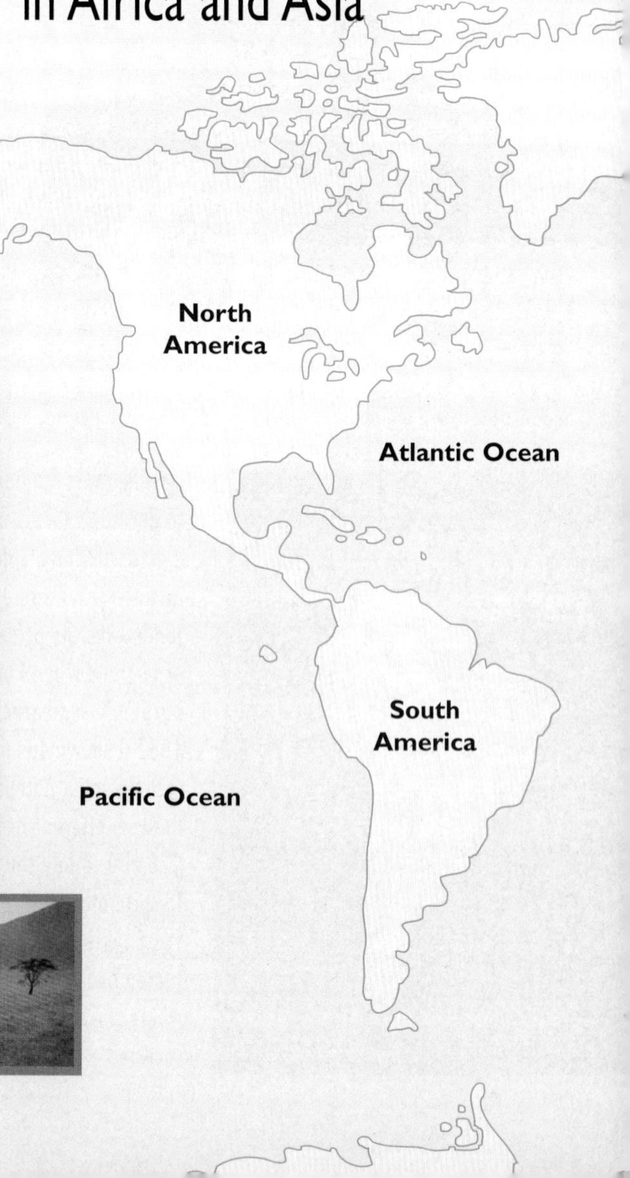

North
America

Atlantic Ocean

South
America

Pacific Ocean

Arctic
Europe
Asia
Africa
Indian Ocean
Australia
Antarctic

Asian elephant
African elephant

ELEPHANTS

Principal Species

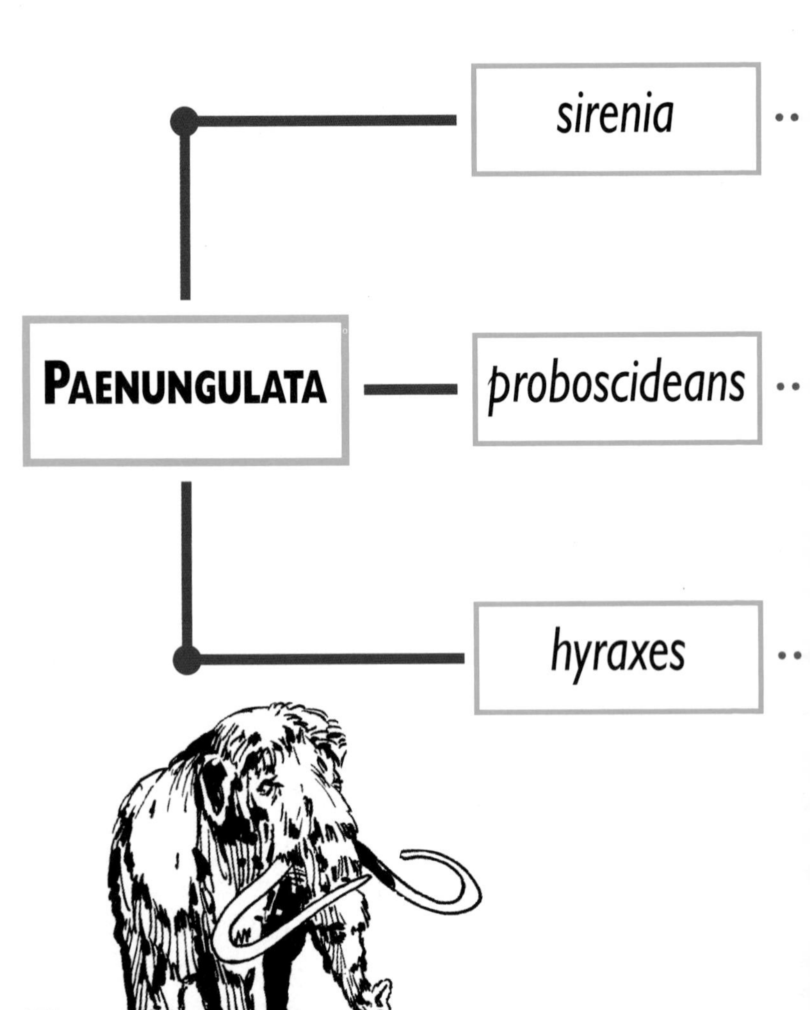

Manatees live in fresh or brackish water. They are probably distant cousins of the elephants.

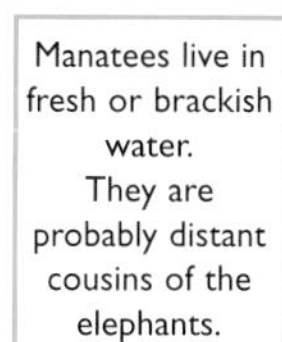

Dugongs are marine mammals and the most widely found species of the sirenia genus.

The untameable African elephant *Loxodonta africana* is the bigger of the two surviving proboscideans.

The Asian elephant, *Elephas maximus*, can be tamed. In Asia, elephants are viewed as sacred and worshipped.

Hyraxes, the smallest relatives of the elephant, survive only on the African continent and in the Middle East.

Moeritherium, mammoth and mastodon have left a trunk and tusks to their present-day descendants.

Creative workshop

Having studied all of these creatures,
it's time to get creative.

All you need are a few odds and ends and a little ingenuity, and you can incorporate some of the animals we've seen into beautiful craft objects.

These simple projects will give you further insight into the animal kingdom presented in the pages of this book.

An original and simple way to enjoy the wonderful images of the animal kingdom.

Elephant Teapot

With a few brush-strokes you can transform a simple teapot into a majestic elephant from the Indies.

Drawing

• Copy the lines of the elephant on the teapot using the felt-tip pen. If you need to correct any lines they can be rubbed out using a finger or a cotton-bud.

Painting

• To paint the elephant as shown, mix ivory and charcoal grey to obtain a strong grey. Apply this mixture with the paintbrush.
• While the paint is drying, paint the whole of the teapot lid except

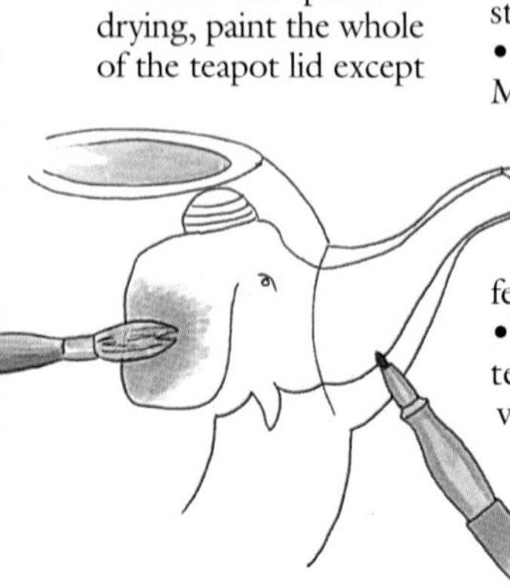

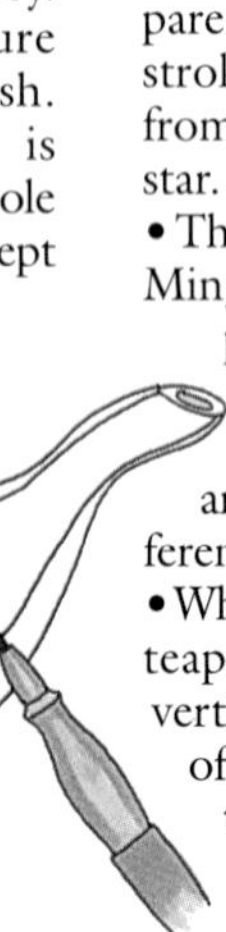

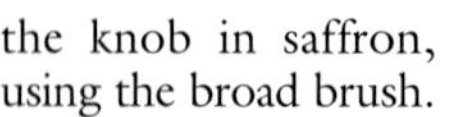

the knob in saffron, using the broad brush. As this colour is fairly transparent, use brush-strokes radiating out from the centre like a star.
• Then paint the knob Ming blue using the paintbrush and add little touches of hematite all around the circumference of the lid.
• When the grey on the teapot is dry, apply vertical brush-strokes of Ming blue using the broad brush to represent the blanket, and Ming blue mixed with saffron using the paintbrush to paint the elephant's hat.
• Paint the tassels and round the edge of the carpet in hematite.

Cloisonné

• Once the paint is dry, have a few trial goes at applying cloisonné on a sheet of paper before attempting the teapot.

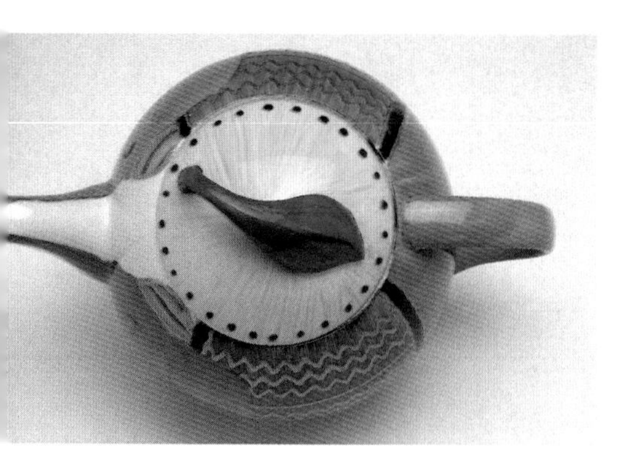

Firing

• Once the cloisonné is dry, place the teapot and its lid in the oven at 150°C, gas mark 3, for 35 minutes. This firing has the advantage of making the colours very bright and the paint very hard-wearing, even in the dishwasher.

• To prevent the line from shaking, make sure the tip of the nozzle does not touch the support; squeeze the paste with steady pressure and draw it out slowly by moving the whole hand over the motif to be drawn. The gold-coloured cloisonné should be applied to the carpet, the hat and the eye.

Materials

• A round white china teapot (must be able to withstand a temperature of 150°C) • Paints for painting on china: charcoal grey, Ming blue, saffron, hematite and ivory
• A broad brush
• A paintbrush
• Gold-coloured cloisonné paste suitable for firing
• A fine black felt-tip pen

Elephant Mirror

This mirror fit for an Indian princess plays on the contrast between the simplicity of the materials used and the rich effect obtained.

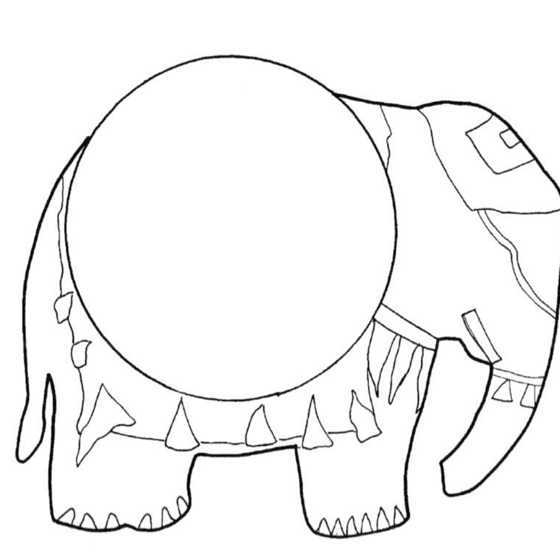

Preparation

• Photocopy the elephant pattern and blow it up to a suitable size to go with the size of your mirror. Using the glue sparingly, stick the photocopy you have made onto the card. Cut round the elephant with the cutter, then remove the paper.

Applying the crepe paper

• Cut strips of brown crepe paper about 3 cm wide. Then tear these strips up to make irregular-shaped scraps of paper like large confetti.

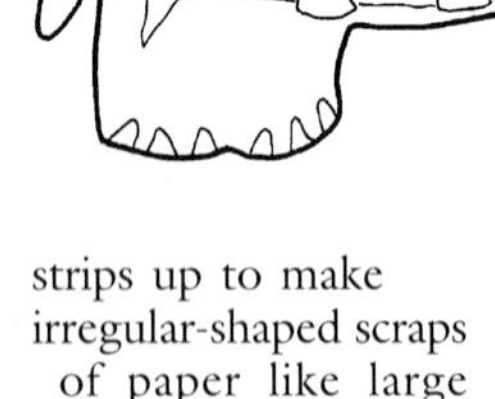

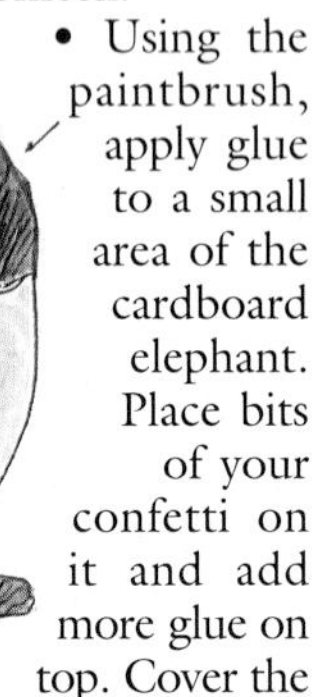

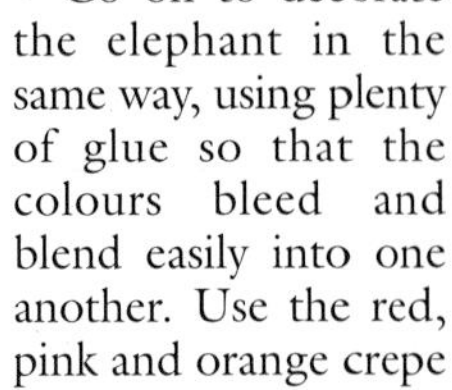

• Using the paintbrush, apply glue to a small area of the cardboard elephant. Place bits of your confetti on it and add more glue on top. Cover the whole of the surface like this, with your scraps of crepe paper stuck down so that they overlap at random, one on top of another. Wait for at least an hour for the brown layer to dry.

• Go on to decorate the elephant in the same way, using plenty of glue so that the colours bleed and blend easily into one another. Use the red, pink and orange crepe

paper to represent the blanket, the braid and the pom-poms. Use beige for the elephant's trunk and toenails.
• Allow to dry overnight.

Fitting the mirror

• Cut a strip of gold crepe paper 2 cm wide and long enough to go right round the mirror. Fold the strip in half along its length and glue it round the circumference of the mirror so as to frame it.
• Stick the mirror as shown, using double-sided adhesive tape or solvent-free glue to avoid dissolving the silvering of the mirror. You can stick a picture-hook to the back to hang up the mirror.

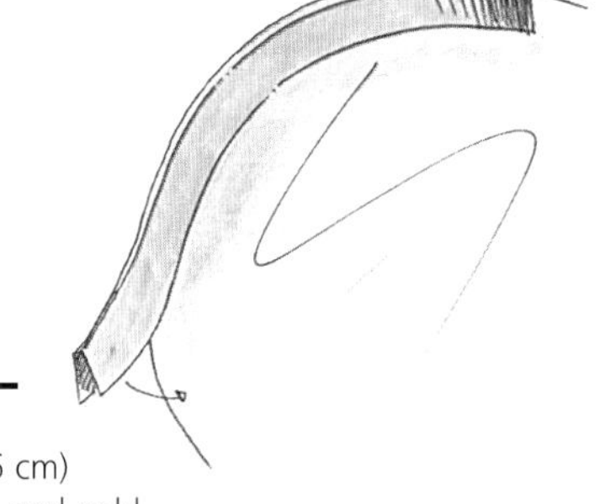

Materials

- A round mirror (here 18 cm in diameter)
- A piece of stiff card 3 mm thick (here 30 x 26 cm)
- Crepe paper: brown, red, orange, pink, beige and gold
- Cellulose glue or thick wallpaper paste
- A flat brush • A cutter
- Solvent-free glue or wide double-sided adhesive tape

Elephant Sculpture

To make this elephant painted with acrylics, you need to build a structure out of cardboard and then coat it in plaster.

For the cardboard model

Photocopy the patterns and blow them up to the sizes shown (in cm). Cut out each one and stick it onto a piece of card, draw round it and remove the paper.
• Cut out the pieces and assemble them, using the adhesive tape to stick them together.

Plastering

• When the structure is finished, gradually cover the elephant with plaster bandages so as to emphasise the contours of the shape you have made. The plaster bandages should be dipped in water one by one and placed over the shape as required.

Painting

• When the plaster is dry, paint the statuette with acrylic paints using blue-grey for the body, slightly darker grey for the ears and ivory white for the tusks. Pick out the eyes in black.

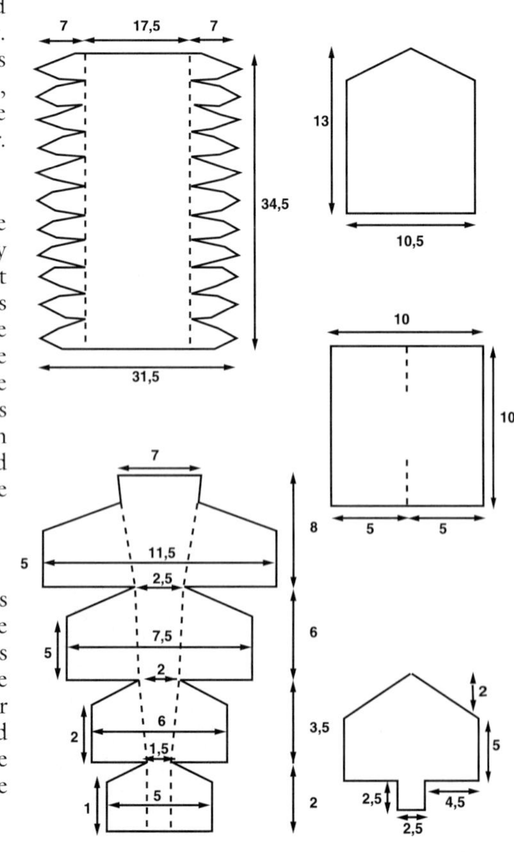

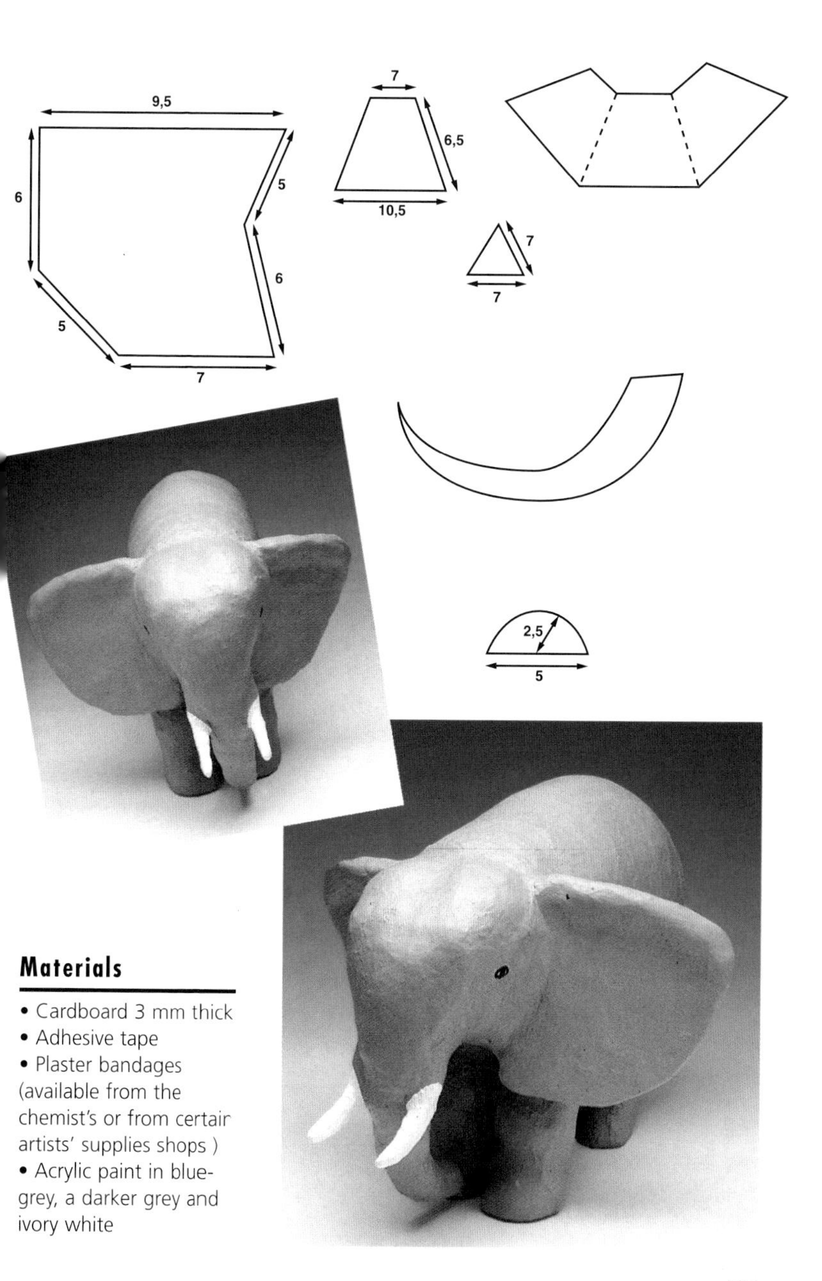

Materials

- Cardboard 3 mm thick
- Adhesive tape
- Plaster bandages (available from the chemist's or from certain artists' supplies shops)
- Acrylic paint in blue-grey, a darker grey and ivory white

‘Night in the Jungle Elephant Lantern

A simple sheet of paper rolled into a cylinder transforms the light of a bare light-bulb into a night-time glow that seems to whisk you off to a faraway land.

Creating the scenery

• Cut a strip of the midnight blue paper card measuring 20 x 30 cm. Make a tracing of the whole scene: the elephant, the trees, the moon etc. making sure that you keep each part of the design in its position in relation to the others. The sky and the ground follow the long sides of the strip.

• Lay the strip flat on the cutting board. Using the cutter, cut round the elephant from point A to point B only, then round the moon from C to D.

• Place the sheet on the felting of an ironing board or place a piece of lightweight felt between it and the cutting board. Hold down the corners with adhesive tape. Prick holes at regular intervals all round the rest of the outline of each part of the design with the awl. Then prick a lot of little dots across the background to represent the stars.

Assembling the lantern

• Roll up the strip of paper with its open-work design to make a cylinder

and fasten with two staples.
Cut a strip of woven raffia cloth 30 x 12 cm. Fray it to make a fringe 8 cm wide all along one edge by pulling the threads on this edge evenly. Staple the strip of raffia around the bottom of the cylinder. To make a more richly decorated lantern you might like to cut a strip 1.5 x 30 cm from a piece of brass sheeting and make little 1.5 cm grooves across it using the awl so that it is striped all along its length. Staple it around the top edge of the cylinder.

Hanging

• To hang up the lantern, staple a 30 cm length of raffia fibre from one edge of the lantern to the other. Fasten this ribbon to the electric flex of the light using the clothes peg or spring clip. Use with a 20 watt bulb maximum.

Materials

• An A3 sheet of midnight blue paper card. • A small piece of woven raffia cloth measuring 12 x 30 cm.
• A 30 cm length of raffia fibre. • An awl and a cutter.
• A cutting board or a sheet of thick cardboard to protect the work-surface on which you cut. • A piece of lightweight felt, flannelette or ironing board felting.
• Neoprene glue.
• A wooden clothes-peg or midnight-blue spring clip. • For a more attractive finish, a piece of fine brass sheeting (from certain arts and crafts shops).

Photographic credits

AKG: 76 - Bondoux Caroline: 102a - CAT'S COLLECTION: 55, 70-71 -
Château-Musée de Dieppe: 114, 119a, 123b -
CHAUMETON: Berthoule: 4, 57a; Chana: 26a; Chaumeton: 23a, 28, 29, 32b, 33a, 35a, 34-35, 127a; Lanceau: 22a; Nature/Fritz Pölking: 6, 7, 8a, 10a, 11a, 14a, 16b, 22b, 129c;
Nature/Grospas: 8b, 9a, 12a, 13a, 15a, 19a, 20a, 21, 126a; Nature/Samba: 27b;
Pho.n.e.: 60-61, 129a; Samba/Chaumeton: 9b, 12-13, 14b, 15b, 19b, 20b, 25b, 126b, 126c -
Collection Panem et Circenses, fonds BONVALLET-JACOB-WILLIAM: 124-125 -
D.R.: 62a, 63b, 74b, 80a, 83a, 83b, 86, 87, 97b, 125a -
EXPLORER: 65; L. Bertrand: 112a; Ginette Cros: 88a; J. Darche: 78a;
Coll. ES: 111b, 116a, 117a; Philippart de Foy: 77b; Stéphane Frances: 95, 98a, 100-101;
Grandadam: 75; G. Kremer: 77c; J.M. Labat: 77a;
Lissac P.: 89b, 90-91, 96; Mattes R.: 64; G. Namur: 117b; Nou J.L.: 92b;
Philippe Roy: 48b, 110b; Tetrel-P.: 47; A. Thomas: 82a; Veiller H.: 89a -
FRALIB/Thé Eléphant: 122b -
GAMMA: 105a; Patrick Aventurier: 94a, 94b, 97a, 101a, 103, 104a, 104b;
Jimmy Bolcina: 85a; Alain Denize: 72a; Thierry Falise: 106-107; François Guenet: 73a;
L. Gubb/Liaison: 74a; Guichard: 107a; Guy Hobbs: 73b, 79a, 81a; Laurent Maous: 84-85;
Mingasson/Liaison: 123a; Anne Nosten: 69b, 70a; J.P. Paireault: 90a;
Eric Pasquier/Saola: 105b, 106a; Stone/Liaison: 78b; J.L. Temporal-Gerfaut: 67, 69a;
Willets/Camerapix: 80-81 -
JACANA: Amsler Kurt: 62b; Cauchoix Denis: 30b; Jean-Pierre Champroux: 59a;
Cordier Sylvain: 24, 50b, 79b; Darmon Olivier: 71a; Dragesco Jean: 18;
Fiore Silvio: 37, 39a, 127b; Frederic: 51a; Gladu Yves: 63a, 129b; Haagner Clem: 59b;
de Klemm Cyril: 60a; Layer Werner: 36a, 36b; Lindblad S.O./HR: 25a;
Philips M./PHR: 58a, 129f; Pisani Sylvie: 32a; Pickford Peter: 66, 68a;
Poulard Jacques: 42a; Renson Geneviève: 23b; Robert Jacques: 56;
Shah Anup: 30a, 31a, 34a, 38, 39b, 40a, 40b, 41a, 41b, 42-43, 43a, 44a, 44b, 45a, 45b, 127c, 129d; Varin Jean-Philippe: 33b, 53a; Varin/Visage: 31b, 61a; Veiller Henri: 10-11;
Wild Pat: 5, 16a, 17, 26b, 27a; Wisniewski Winfried: 2;
Walz Uwe-GDT : 131; Wu Norbert : 58b -
KINGFISHER: 46, 48a, 49a, 50a, 52b, 53b, 54a, 57b, 82b, 91a, 109, 116b, 119b, 122a, 129e -
Lemaire Nicolas: 92a, 93b -
Musée de Brou, Bourg-en-Bresse: "Bataille d'Alexandre", Fontebasso: 115a -
Musée Paul Dupuy, Toulouse: Olifant dit "Cor de Roland": 118 -
Indian Tourist Office: 98b -
Thai Tourist Office: 99a, 99b, 100a -
Sri Lankan Tourist Office: 102b -
Palais des Beaux-Arts de Lille: "Bataille d'Alexandre et de Poros",
François Watteau (1758-1823), photo Ph. Bernard: 112b- Sun International: 84a -
ROGER-VIOLLET: 52a, 68b, 72b, 115b, 120-121 - WALT-DISNEY: 108, 124a -

Front cover: JACANA: Robert Jacques - Lemaire Nicolas: a - WALT DISNEY: b
Back cover: Sun International: a - D.R.: b - JACANA: Cordier Sylvain: c -
GAMMA: Aventurier Patrick: d

Acknowledgements:

The publishers would like to thank all those who have contributed to this book, in particular:
Guy-Claude Agboton, Evelyne-Alice Bridier, Antoine Caron, Jean-Jacques Carreras, Michèle Forest, Céline Gerst, Rizlane Lazrak, Nicolas Lemaire, Hervé Levano, Marie-Bénédicte Majoral, Kha Luan Pham, Vincent Pompougnac, Marie-Laure Sers-Besson, Emmanuèle Zumstein

Illustration: Frantz Rey

Translation: Kate Clayton, Judith Hayward - Ros Schwartz Translations

Impression: Eurolitho - Milan
Dépôt légal: September 1998
Printed in Italy